PERGOLAS
ARBOURS·GAZEBOS
FOLLIES

PERGOLAS
ARBOURS·GAZEBOS
FOLLIES

DAVID STEVENS

WARD LOCK

This paperback edition
first published in Great Britain
in 1991 by Ward Lock Limited,
Villiers House, 41–47 Strand,
London WC2N 5JE, a Cassell company.

House editor Denis Ingram
Text set in Caledonia
by MS Filmsetting Limited, Frome, Somerset

Printed and bound in Spain
by Graficas Reunidas

British Library Cataloguing in Publication Data
Stevens, David, *1943–*
    Pergolas, arbours, gazebos and follies.
    1. Gardens——Design 2. Garden structures
    I. Title
    <u>717</u>   SB472

ISBN 0-7063-6992-0

Contents

Preface 6
1 Design considerations 8
2 Arbours and overheads 16
3 Pergolas and arches 46
4 Gazebos 79
5 Follies 109
Index 126
Acknowledgements 128

Preface

Simplicity is the key to good design and nowhere is this more apparent than in the garden. The problem with such a basic rule is how to relate it to an inherently complicated subject, a subject that is full of ever changing patterns that rely on the turning seasons, the vagaries of the climate and not least the gardener's own personality.

It is of course the last that holds the key to any composition. It is here that the basic garden components are resolved; room to sit, paths for access, buildings for storage or greenhouses for growing, lawns, trees, plants and vegetables. All of these will be honed into a particular pattern, reflecting an individual character and underlining the point that no two plots can ever be identical. While such components are the backbone of a design it is planting and ornamentation that really brings things together. No garden is complete without these, but the prime consideration, particularly with the latter, is their utilization in a sensible, coherent and not least elegant manner. A surfeit of focal points is not only restless but boring. Good design is quite the opposite, relying on positive statements allied to a degree of surprise that can lead both feet and eye through what is essentially an outdoor room, in a most delightful way.

The scope of this book is to look at what are essentially the larger ornamental structures within the garden framework. In fact, as far as pergolas are concerned, they may well provide all or part of that framework. It is also true that there is nothing new in gardening and from the very earliest times arches and overhead beams have been vital for the training of vines and other plants to provide both food and shelter from a powerful sun. In so doing they naturally spanned paths and provided division, becoming essential parts of the garden plan.

Equally it could be argued that man's earliest dwellings were within caves, a subject returned to with considerable enthusiasm in the great landscape parks of the eighteenth century. Then grottoes were something of a passion for gentlemen with extravagant tastes, financial obesity and a sense of humour to match. You might be forgiven for thinking that such whims were the preserve of a bygone era but not so. A particularly charming client of mine had me construct a grotto within his grounds, complete with hired hermit who, clothed in a tailor-made robe of hessian, would, for a substantial retainer, regale astonished guests with quotes from *Paradise Lost*.

Gazebos on the other hand are far from impractical. They are quite simply rooms with a view, so their location is of paramount importance. Again they have historical significance and their history runs roughly parallel with follies. Such delightful little buildings were strategically placed to look in or out of a garden and over the years their kin has come down to us in the form of summer-houses, which should always be free standing and never tacked on to a building in the form of a conservatory.

So whether it be folly, gazebo, pergola or arch, history has taken a firm hand in their development. Today's problem, however, is not so much how to recreate these visual delights, but how to remove them from their grand ancestral setting and find a place for them in the altogether more constricted confines of a modern garden. This is far from easy as commercial pressures have in many instances reduced all of them to a travesty of their former glory. Follies became pixie cottages, gazebos ridiculous alpine summer-houses, while pergolas and arches can be seen in a thousand garden centres as tortured extrusions of plastic-coated wire. The mighty have indeed fallen, but thankfully not without a degree of hope. The basic concept of all these remains alive and well, and continues to be constructed by professional garden architects and gifted amateurs up and down the country.

Another joy is that they have all become a thoroughly indigenous part of the English garden scene. It is true that you can see likenesses all over the world, but for my money a lazy arbour decorated in high summer with hollyhocks and climbing roses, or a starkly realistic ruin looming out of a Hampshire mist, have a ring of truth that refreshes me whenever I return from working overseas. My own enthusiasm for the subject stems from a formal training in landscape architecture and an increasingly varied career spanning more than fifteen years. Throughout this time one slowly gains an insight not only of the vast range of styles and idiosyncrasies that have been built, but also the way in which they can be used in a contemporary setting.

English garden design is in a state of flux, sweeping away many of the fussy conventions beloved by the Victorians. In many ways it is returning to the simplicity of those great landscape parks, albeit on a smaller scale and altogether different criteria. Such change has already profoundly affected both the American and Scandinavian approach to living outside. Theirs is an uncluttered and, some would say, clinical style. In this country we are moving in the same direction but the end results are neither so austere nor so simple. The English are by nature individualistic in their approach to gardening and, almost certainly, always retain a fondness for ornamentation in all its guises.

Whether your interest is historical or contemporary, the content of this book is fascinating. In many ways the subject is also unusual, and as someone engaged in the landscape design profession, I learnt a great deal during its preparation. This fact alone convinces me that follies, gazebos, pergolas and arches have an increasingly important role to play in the garden. Look at the options, refrain from slavish mimicry and produce something that reflects your own personality; the result will delight you.

D.S.

1

Design Considerations

THE IMPORTANCE OF PLANNING

I always find it rather odd that although most people are quite capable of planning the inside of their homes, the outside seems to get forgotten. Not always, to be sure, for there are some delightful examples of good design where house and garden are treated as a single entity, the one flowing on and out from the other. Why some people should be better at this than their neighbours has little to do with formal training, or even botanical knowledge. The worst culprits are often architects and for the life of me I can never understand how the rhythm and obvious competence of a good working drawing can degenerate into a meaningless jumble of unrelated features outside the confines of four walls.

Garden planning relies heavily on commonsense, as does all good design, and there is absolutely no credence in the belief that designers conjure inspiration from thin air. Any architect, landscape or otherwise, works from a set of well tested rules that he or she knows will generate a degree of success, although this should never preclude original thinking and genuine inspiration which is often born of experience. Such talent can lift one from straightforward ability into an altogether far higher plane. From my own point of view I always strive for excellence and am usually satisfied with the end product, after more or less work. There is no doubt however that on occasion things come together in a different way that makes me glow with enthusiasm in the certain knowledge that there is something more involved than plain competence.

Hypothetical self-congratulation is all very well but what we really want to know is how to plan our garden in basic terms and, more importantly, locate the features that are the subject of this book. To do this an understanding of a few basic design rules is essential.

The trouble with most of us is that we are governed by impulse rather than anything else and this means that on the first fine day in spring we rush to the nearest garden centre, buy a bootful of paving, pots, plants and assorted goodies and subsequently arrange these in some state of disarray in the garden. Such outings more often than not happen at irregular intervals throughout the year and produce results that, while perhaps pleasing, lack any real purpose and almost certainly fail to realize the full potential of your 'outdoor room'. Focal points and features are of course an integral part of all this, but by their very nature they need careful siting and cannot be just slapped down anywhere. If they are, the picture is confused and they lose their inherent strength.

Perhaps one of the most important elements of garden planning is therefore patience, or at least a degree of restraint.

Having run a landscape planning service for a national magazine for many years, I have evolved a straightforward questionnaire that allows all relevant information to be put together on a single sheet of paper. It is divided into two sections and asks quite simply 'what have you got?', and 'what do you want?'.

WHAT HAVE YOU GOT?

This question involves a very basic survey to check the overall dimensions of the plot, any changes of level, the direction of prevailing winds, position of existing features that might include trees and planting, types of boundary fencing, etc. It should also include the north point (or where the sun shines at midday), the possibility of good or, more likely, bad views and any other factors both within or outside the garden that might impinge on the layout.

Without going into the technicalities of surveying, be sure to use a long tape and take this from one side and then one end to the other, jotting down 'running' measurements as you go. Never try to measure from point to point in isolation, the outcome can be most confusing! A very simple survey takes all these factors into account, and when this is converted into a scale drawing on graph paper it will not only form the basis for an accurate design but will obviate the danger-ous practice of creating compositions on the back of envelopes, a sure recipe for disaster. Such a survey applies equally well to a brand new plot or an established garden that may well need modification and, where the latter is concerned, be sure to indicate all planting however unpromising this may seem.

As an indication of how important this is, I was working on a garden recently that was straddled by an ancient and unkempt black-thorn hedge. The owners were convinced that this should go, it being part of an older garden that had been divided into building plots. With careful thinning and pruning however, I managed to work it into the new design so successfully that it became not only a natural division but also a frame for a newly created view beyond. This was living sculp-ture, a screen, pergola and arch all rolled into one and what's more it was free! It could have served equally well as a backdrop for any kind of building, including a gazebo or even, at a pinch, a quaint but not impractical frame for a folly.

At this stage, however, one is not even considering such ideas. These come much later on, and certainly not before the survey has been transferred to a scale drawing. To do this, take a sheet of graph paper and use a simple measurement of, say, one square per foot, or five squares per metre. Mark in all those things shown on the survey and when you have finished take one or two photocopies

that act as an insurance against losing the original. Our survey has been transferred to a scale drawing as shown in Fig. 1. You can see that it is a very average plot measuring 33.5 m × 9 m (110 ft × 30 ft). It has an awk-ward apex at the top, a number of old fruit trees and is uncompromisingly flat. It has the advantage of facing south but is typical of thousands of contemporaries that we pass on the train when entering any large city.

WHAT DO YOU WANT?

Such a garden, apart from having to fulfil the normal functions of a terrace for sitting and dining, can incorporate any number of per-sonal requirements. These might include bar-becues, pools, sandpits, vegetables, lawn, planting and many other items. Not only do any or all of these have to fit in somewhere, but they have to blend into an overall compo-sition that provides a feeling of space and movement, detracting from boundaries that are almost inevitably rectangular.

In our situation we have chosen to illus-trate the importance of a series of focal points that lead one down the garden creating 'pools' of interest. It also proves the point that although under normal circumstances one would not consider using *all* the subjects of this book, it can not only be achieved but also brought about in such a way as to provide a fascinating perspective.

Moving away from the house, the paved area is of ample size and utilizes a combin-ation of neat precast slabs and brick, the latter helping to soften the overall surface as well as providing a visual link with the adjoin-ing building. The paving pattern is designed to lead the eye diagonally across the space, opening up the latter and tying the built-in seat into the overall composition. On the other side of the terrace the raised bed and herbs echo the interlocking brick rectangles, the low aromatic plants being framed by an equally fragrant clipped lavender hedge. Lin-

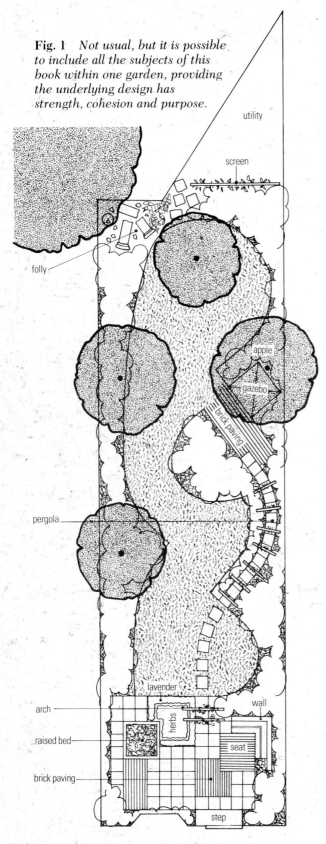

Fig. 1 *Not usual, but it is possible to include all the subjects of this book within one garden, providing the underlying design has strength, cohesion and purpose.*

king the two sides of the terrace and acting as both a gateway and frame to the garden beyond is the first of our garden features, a simple archway smothered with a perfumed honeysuckle. In isolation the arch would not be effective, but reinforced as it is by the combination of planting, seat and raised bed it forms a focus and 'tension point' that leads both feet and eye in a preconceived direction.

With what is essentially a long narrow garden we need to emphasize the inherent width of the plot at the expense of the length and, to do this, the path that leads on from the arch swings away to the right-hand side in a gentle curve. Another task, and another essential component of any good garden design, is to create a feeling of mystery, preventing the overall concept from being seen in its entirety from any single viewpoint. In order to reinforce this, our path slides away softly under a pergola, from light to dappled shade, and continues on its way with a series of fragmented views that increase the visual space and encourage one on towards the end of the tunnel and the next 'outdoor room'.

A gazebo is quite simply a room with a view. It is not a summer-house, shed, conservatory or battered lean-to that may be tacked onto the rear of a house as an afterthought to satisfy a family whim. It serves a visual pleasure and in our garden acts as a punctuation mark at the end of the path and pergola. Such a feature – any feature for that matter – must have a positive place to go. A surfeit of focal points is restless, a dearth is boring. In this design the building sits comfortably to one side, roughly equidistant between the terrace and bottom boundary. It has been positioned carefully to be viewed from and have a view back towards the house. By being to one side rather than in the middle of the space it sets up a diagonal axis and this creates a feeling of greater space, a diagonal line always being the longest across any

This eccentric house extension is a genuine attempt to produce a restless and bizarre end result – in the best tradition of contemporary follies.